Espresso *Magic*

by Kymberly Martin and Dennis Martin

Illustrations by: Donna Bernard
Cover design by: David Shadle

Sixth Edition
Revised Edition Printing 1991
Copyrighted © March 1989
By Kymberly Martin and Dennis Martin

ISBN # 0-9631850-0-4

Printed in the United States of America

Published by:
Shady Lane Enterprises
P.O. Box 55942
Lake Forest Park, WA. 98155

Published by: **Shady Lane Enterprises**

Shady Lane Enterprises
P.O.Box 55942
Lake Forest Park, WA
98155

Table of Contents

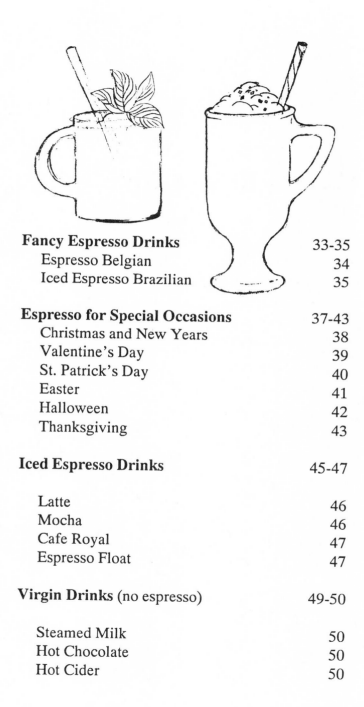

Fancy Espresso Drinks
33-35

    Espresso Belgian   34
    Iced Espresso Brazilian   35

Espresso for Special Occasions
37-43

    Christmas and New Years   38
    Valentine's Day   39
    St. Patrick's Day   40
    Easter   41
    Halloween   42
    Thanksgiving   43

Iced Espresso Drinks
45-47

    Latte   46
    Mocha   46
    Cafe Royal   47
    Espresso Float   47

Virgin Drinks (no espresso)
49-50

    Steamed Milk   50
    Hot Chocolate   50
    Hot Cider   50

Kym's Love Cup

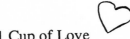

- 1 Cup of Love
- 4 ozs of Kisses
- 1/2 oz of Teasing
- 1/2 oz of Squeezing

Combine above ingredients

Stir in laughter

Garnish with plenty of sunshine

Congratulations, you now have the opportunity to create exciting espresso drinks in your home. You have previously experienced the enjoyment of an espresso; savored the rich, robust, distinctive taste in a mall or cafe. That special good as-it-smells taste of espresso can now be made at your leisure.

Espresso starts by grinding fresh, natural coffee beans and with a few moments of preparation you enjoy a drink that is magical.

This collection of Espresso Magic recipes will help you prepare your favorite espresso drinks and discover new ones. Some you will want to share, and others may be just right for you. Espresso is made to suit the taste and mood. Like a fine wine, espresso complements the occasion.

Espresso is more than just a cup of coffee. Espresso is actually several things:

- an extremely dark coffee roast
- a fine gritty grind
- a method of brewing

Brewed correctly these three items bring out the very essence of the coffee. Espresso creates a special atmosphere appreciated by many the world over. Each cup of espresso is usually ground and brewed individually to suit personal taste. The more adventuresome will experiment by adding different flavorings. A dash of your favorite liqueur or syrup will add that personal touch. The amounts given in the following recipes are guides. Use more or less of the ingredients to suit your own taste. Satisfaction makes espresso an experience. You have the freedom to be creative and try different ingredients.

The key ingredient, however, is the type of coffee bean used. The coffee beans provide a foundation for the espresso drink being prepared. Espresso roast is commonly used, but try other dark roasts. Any type of dark roast may be brewed in an espresso machine. French Vanilla is an excellent flavored coffee to try; the darkness of French roast creates a rich espresso while the flavor adds a touch of vanilla. Other specialty blends are also available.

Vienna blend is popular among espresso drinkers. A visit to a local coffee supplier will make you aware of the many coffee beans available from around the world.

Immediately before preparing espresso, grind the beans to a fine gritty texture. This assures that the essence of the bean is transferred to the espresso drink.

Pack the freshly ground beans down in the receptacle just hard enough so the water is forced through the coffee slowly. It is a sensitive balance; the **texture** and **packing** of the ground coffee determines the **time** required for the water to be forced through . If the grind is too fine or packed too hard the water may not be forced through. If the grind is too coarse or not packed down hard enough the water will rush through producing a bitter, watery liquid.

If a plastic tamping tool was not provided with your espresso machine, don't despair. Try using a 1/3 measuring cup or one that fits the receptacle.

Avoid overbrewing. The essence of the coffee comes out at the beginning of the brewing process and becomes thinner and more bitter as brewing continues. Brew only the amount of coffee that you will immediately serve.

A golden head of froth is nature's way of telling you that you have brewed a perfect espresso. Your reward is a rich, full-bodied espresso which captures the very heart of the coffee bean.

Steaming Milk

The degree of success you experience in frothing the milk will vary with the type of espresso machine you use and the amount of practice you get. A few suggestions to help you froth milk:

- Use a **cold** <u>stainless steel pitcher</u>.

- Cold two percent milk will froth more easily than whole milk.

Start with the steam tube deep in the milk. Gently open the valve until a strong, steady flow of steam escapes into the milk. Lower the pitcher so that the end of the steam tube is just below the surface of the milk and maintains a steady hissing sound. A rumbling sound means the tube is too deep in the milk. As the froth builds up, maintain the steam tube just below the surface.

When you build up a sufficient head of froth, heat the rest of the milk by lowering the steam tube deep into the pitcher. Prevent burning the milk by slowly moving the pitcher.

Continue to heat the milk to the desired serving temperature. The hand holding the pitcher will feel the heat build up.

- Never boil the milk.

A helpful hint to clean the film of milk that builds up on the steam tube: fill a cup with soda water, Seven-Up, Sprite or Coke. Insert the steam tube into the soda water. As it soaks, the CO_2 will dissolve the milk film.

A. Start with the steam tube deep in the milk before turning on the steam.

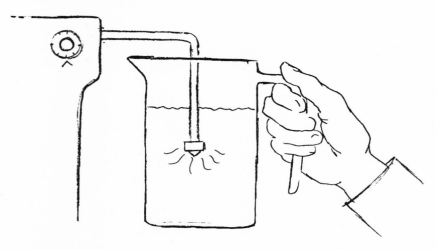

C. As froth builds up, maintain the steam tube just below the surface.

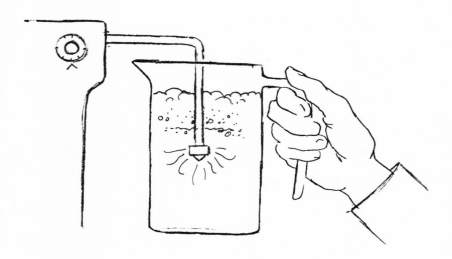

B. Lower the pitcher so that the end of the steam tube is just below the surface.

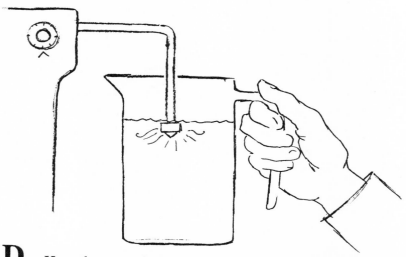

D. Heat the rest of the milk by lowering the steam tube deep into the pitcher. The hand holding the pitcher will feel the heat build up.

Toppings

Make each espresso drink special, by adding a little garnish. Besides accenting the drink, garnish provides the server with visual means of differentiating the drinks. Top off a Mocha with a dollop of whipped cream and a sprinkle of grated chocolate. Accent an Almond Latte with a dollop of foamed milk. Some of the more enhancing toppings are:

sweet ground cocoa

vanilla powder

ground cinnamon

ground nutmeg

orange peel

lemon peel

15

The Basic Espresso Drinks

Use the basic espresso as a foundation to build Cappuccinos, Lattes and Mochas.

Espresso and Espresso Romano

Approximately 2 level tablespoons of espresso ground coffee per demitasse, or as much coffee as needed to fill the receptacle of your particular machine. Typically the yield is between 2-3 ounces of Espresso.

One shot of espresso served in a demitasse cup is a regular espresso. Add milk and sugar to suit your taste. An espresso served with a lemon wedge is Espresso Romano. The lemon wedge helps to blunt the pure robust taste of espresso.

Many first time espresso drinkers are not accustomed to the smooth, full robust taste of the Espresso blend; it is in sharp contrast to pre-ground "American roasted", canned coffee. The typical canned coffee blend found on the supermarket shelves is a light roast that produces an acid taste. Darker espresso roasts have a strong bittersweet taste, sometimes described as nutty, with no hint of acid. Darker roasts lose much of the acid and some caffeine during the roasting process.

Americano

A single shot of espresso in a coffee mug. Add boiling water to the espresso to suit taste.

Espresso Ristretto

Short espresso, the flow of espresso is cut short at about 1 oz. producing a very dense cup of coffee. This will get you going in the morning.

Long Espresso

Flow of espresso is prolonged, producing an extra ounce of espresso. Be especially careful not to overbrew.

Doppio

Double espresso, two demitasse espressos combine to make one drink. Most espresso drinks may be made with a double or single shot.

Tall

Tall means one shot of espresso, served in a larger cup. It is not to be confused with the Long Espresso. Usually milk or water is added to suit the taste. The more milk or water added to an espresso, the more the flavor is subdued.

Basic Espresso with Regular Coffee

This will add extra zest to your regular coffee.

Pile Driver

A shot of espresso in a regular coffee mug and topped off with your favorite coffee.

Layered

A shot of espresso in a regular coffee mug, filled half full with your favorite coffee and topped with steamed milk.

Layered with Flavor

A shot of espresso in a regular coffee mug, filled half full with your favorite coffee. Add a flavoring to suit your taste and top it off with steamed milk.

Espresso with Liqueur

Around the world, coffee means hospitality and there is nothing better than the aromas of liqueurs and brandies and espresso blended and served for an after-dinner relaxing beverage.

It is recommended that you preheat your cups or glasses with steam. Add spirits to the cup or glass first then the espresso. Add flavorings, sugar to taste and toppings or garnish. Use fresh whipped cream as aerosol cream will melt when it tops the hot espresso.

For iced drinks, add ice in a tall glass or blend in blender and make a frothy cooler.

Cafe Anisette

- 2-3 ounces of espresso
- 1 Tbs of anisette
- a lemon wedge

Pour one shot of espresso into a demitasse cup; add 1 Tbs of anisette. Serve with a wedge of lemon.

Cafe Seville

- 2-3 ounces of espresso
- 1 Tbs of Cointreau
- an orange twist

Pour one shot of espresso into a demitasse cup; add 1 Tbs of Cointreau, garnish with an orange twist and sweeten to taste.

Espresso Amaretto

- 2-3 ounces of espresso
- 1 Tbs of Amaretto
- an orange twist

Pour 1 Tbs of amaretto in demitasse cup; fill with espresso, garnish with an orange twist and sweeten to taste.

Cappuccino

Cappuccino

- 2-3 ounces of espresso
- 3/4 cup of foamed milk

Pour a single shot of espresso into a cappuccino cup. Add three quarters of a cup of foamed milk. It is helpful to use a spoon to scoop the foam from the pitcher.

Latteccino

- 2-3 ounces of espresso
- 1/3 cup of steamed milk
- 1/3 cup of foamed milk

Pour a shot of espresso into a cappuccino cup or coffee mug; add half steamed milk, then half foamed milk. Served in a clear glass coffee mug, this drink creates eye appealing layers.

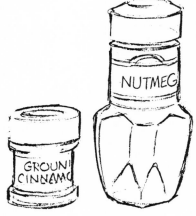

Latte

A Latte is single shot of espresso in a coffee mug with steamed milk added. Use a spoon to hold back the foam and pour the steamed milk into the mug, leaving just enough room to put a spoonful of foam on top. You may stir in flavored syrup or sweeteners. Lattes are a favorite way of preparing espresso. It is important that the milk not be boiled or burned (see steaming milk).

Almond Latte

- 2-3 ounces of espresso
- 2/3 cup of steamed milk
- 1-2 Tbs of foamed milk
- 2 Tablespoons of orgeat syrup
- a pinch of slivered almonds

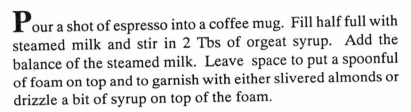

Pour a shot of espresso into a coffee mug. Fill half full with steamed milk and stir in 2 Tbs of orgeat syrup. Add the balance of the steamed milk. Leave space to put a spoonful of foam on top and to garnish with either slivered almonds or drizzle a bit of syrup on top of the foam.

Vanilla Latte

- 2-3 ounces of espresso
- 2/3 cup of steamed milk
- 1-2 Tbs of foam milk
- 3 Tbs of vanilla syrup
- a pinch of vanilla powder

Pour a shot of espresso into a coffee mug. Fill half way with steamed milk, stir in 3 Tbs of vanilla syrup. Add the balance of the steamed milk, leaving space to put a spoonful of foamed milk on top and to sprinkle a bit of vanilla powder over the foam.

Hazelnut Latte

- 2-3 ounces of espresso
- 2/3 cup of steamed milk
- 1-2 Tbs of foamed milk
- 3 Tbs of hazelnut syrup
- a pinch of vanilla powder

Pour a shot of espresso into a coffee mug. Fill half full with steamed milk, stir in 3 Tbs of hazelnut syrup. Add the balance of the steamed milk, leaving space to put a spoonful of foam on top and to sprinkle a bit of vanilla powder or drizzle a bit of syrup over the foam.

Vanilla Nut Latte

- 2-3 ounces of espresso
- 2/3 cup of steamed milk
- 1-2 Tbs of foamed milk
- 2 Tbs of vanilla syrup

- 1 Tbs of orgeat syrup
or
- 2 Tbs of hazelnut syrup
- a pinch of vanilla powder
- a pinch of slivered almonds

This very tasty drink can be made two ways. Pour a shot of espresso into a coffee mug. Fill half full with steamed milk. Stir in 2 Tbs of vanilla and either 1 Tbs of orgeat syrup or 2 Tbs of hazelnut syrup and add balance of the steamed milk. Leave room to put a spoonful of foam on top and sprinkle a bit of vanilla powder and almond slivers over the foam.

Cafe Mocha

- 2-3 ounces of espresso
- 2/3 cup of steamed milk

- 4 Tbs of creme de cacao
  or
- 4 Tbs of Hershey's syrup

  - 1-2 Tbs of whipped cream
  - a pinch of powdered or grated chocolate

If chocolate is what you enjoy this is the espresso drink for you. Serve in a regular coffee mug with a shot of espresso and 4 Tbs of either creme de cacao syrup or Hershey's syrup; fill almost to the top of the mug with steamed milk. Stir and top off with whipped cream, powdered chocolate or grated chocolate.

Cafe Almond Mocha

- 2-3 ounces of espresso
- 2/3 cup of steamed milk

- 4 Tbs of creme de cacao
  or
- 4 Tbs of Hershey's syrup

- 1 Tbs of orgeat syrup
- 1-2 Tbs of whipped cream
- a pinch of almond slivers
- a pinch of powder or grated chocolate

Pour a shot of espresso into a coffee mug, fill half full with steamed milk. Add 4 Tbs of creme de cacao syrup or Hershey's syrup. Add 1 Tbs of orgeat syrup. Stir and fill almost to the top with the balance of the steamed milk. Top off with whipping cream, almond slivers and grated or powdered chocolate.

Vanilla Nut Mocha

- 2-3 ounces of espresso
- 2/3 cup of steamed milk

- 4 Tbs of creme de cacao
  or
- 4 Tbs of Hershey's syrup

- 1 Tbs of orgeat syrup
  or
- 2 Tbs of hazelnut syrup

- 1 Tbs of vanilla syrup
- 1-2 Tbs of whipped cream
- a pinch of powdered or grated chocolate
- a pinch of vanilla powder

A Vanilla Nut Mocha can be made with different ingredients. Pour a shot of espresso into a coffee mug, fill half full with steamed milk. Add 4 Tbs of creme de cacao or Hershey's syrup and 1 Tbs of orgeat syrup; 2 Tbs of hazelnut syrup and 1 Tbs of vanilla syrup. Stir and fill almost to the top of the mug with the balance of the steamed milk, top off with whipping cream. Garnish with vanilla powder and grated chocolate.

Breve

- 2-3 ounces of espresso
- 2/3 cup of steamed cream

Pour a single shot of espresso in a coffee mug. Steamed cream is then added to the espresso creating a very rich drink (due to the density of cream it is very difficult to create foam).

Breve Mocha

- 2-3 ounces of espresso
- 2/3 cup of steamed cream
- 2 Tbs of Hershey's chocolate syrup
- a pinch of powdered chocolate

Pour a single shot of espresso in a regular coffee mug. Fill half full with steamed cream. Add 2 Tbs of Hershey's chocolate syrup; stir and fill to the top with steamed cream. Sprinkle powdered chocolate on top.

Almond Breve

- 2-3 ounces of espresso
- 2/3 cup of steamed cream
- 2 Tbs of orgeat syrup
- a pinch of powdered vanilla

Pour a single shot of espresso in a regular coffee mug. Fill half full with steamed cream. Add 2 Tbs of orgeat syrup; stir and fill to the top with steamed cream. Garnish with powdered vanilla.

Cafe Royal

- 2-3 ounces of espresso
- 2/3 of a cup of steamed condensed milk

Pour a single shot of espresso into a regular coffee mug. Fill to the top with steamed condensed milk. This espresso drink is very sweet; it is not recommended to add any flavored syrup.

Fancy Espresso Drinks

Espresso Belgian

Makes six servings

- 6 shots of espresso
- 2 egg whites
- 1/2 pint of heavy sweet cream
- 4 heaping Tbs of powder sugar
- 1/4 teaspoon of vanilla

Beat egg whites until stiff. In a separate bowl beat the cream until it peaks. Add sugar and vanilla, continue beating until stiff. Gently fold whipped cream into egg whites. Do not substitute canned whipped cream as it melts immediately on contact with the hot coffee.

Fill 6 ounce cups half full with the cream mixture

Top with espresso.

Iced Espresso Brazilian

- 2 squares bitter chocolate
- 2 shots of espresso
- a pinch of salt
- 2 Tbs of sugar
- 3 cups of milk
- whipped cream

Melt 2 squares of bitter chocolate in a double boiler. Add 2 shots of espresso, stirring constantly. Add a pinch of salt and 2 Tbs of sugar, stirring constantly. Add 3 cups of milk; continue stirring until hot. Beat to a froth with a whisk or egg beater. Cool. Pour over cracked ice in tall glasses and top with whipped cream.

Espresso
for
Special
Occasions

Seasonal Drinks

New Years and Christmas

Eggnog Latte

- 2-3 ounces of espresso
- 1/2 cup of eggnog
- 1/8 cup of milk
- cinnamon
- nutmeg

- 2 Tbs of rum *
    or
- 2 Tbs of liqueur *

Since eggnog is readily available in stores the Eggnog Latte makes a perfect holiday drink. In a seasonal mug pour a shot of espresso. Combine eggnog and milk in pitcher and steam. Fill mug half full with eggnog and milk mixture and stir. Fill to brim with eggnog and milk mixture; garnish with cinnamon and nutmeg.

*   Rum or Frangelico liqueur may be added prior to the steamed eggnog mixture to give an extra flavor.

Valentine's Day

Strawberry Latte

- 2-3 ounces of espresso
- 2/3 cup steamed milk
- 3 Tbs strawberry syrup
- 1-2 Tbs whipping cream
- 1 strawberry for garnish

Pour a shot of espresso into a coffee mug. Fill mug half full with steamed milk. Add 3 Tbs of strawberry syrup and stir. Fill almost to the top with steamed milk. Top off with whipping cream and a strawberry cut partially down the middle, placed on the rim of the mug, drizzle a bit of the strawberry syrup on top of the whipping cream.

St. Patrick's Day

Cafe Mocha Mint

- 2-3 ounces of espresso
- 2/3 cup steamed milk
- 2 Tbs creme de menthe

- 3 Tbs creme de cacao
  or
- 3 Tbs Hershey's syrup

- 1-2 Tbs whipping cream
- Pinch of grated chocolate

In a seasonal coffee mug pour a single shot of espresso. Fill half full with steamed milk. Add 2 Tbs of creme de menthe and 3 Tbs of creme de cacao or Hershey's Syrup. Stir and fill almost to the top with steamed milk. Top with whipping cream, drizzle a bit of creme de menthe syrup on top of the whipping cream, and dust with grated chocolate.

Easter

Mint Latte

- 3-4 ounces of espresso
- 2/3 cup steamed milk
- 1-2 Tbs of whipping cream
- 4 Tbs of creme de menthe syrup

In a seasonal coffee mug pour a double shot of espresso. Fill half full with steamed milk. Add 4 Tbs of creme de menthe syrup. Stir and fill almost to the top with steamed milk. Top off with whipping cream and drizzle a bit of creme de menthe syrup.

Halloween

Chocolate Orange Latte

- 2-3 ounces of espresso
- 2/3 cup steamed milk
- 1-2 Tbs of whipping cream
- 1 Tbs of orange syrup
- 1 orange slice

- 2 Tbs of creme de coco
  or
- 2 Tbs Hershey's syrup

In a seasonal coffee mug pour a shot of espresso, fill half full with steamed milk, 1 Tbs of orange syrup, 2 Tbs of creme de cacao or hershey's syrup. Stir and fill almost to the top with steamed milk. Top off with whipping cream, grated chocolate and place an orange slice on the rim of the mug.

Thanksgiving

Viennese

- 2-3 ounces of espresso
- 2/3 cup steamed milk
- 1-2 Tbs of foamed milk
- 1 Teaspoon of cinnamon
- 1 cinnamon stick

In a seasonal coffee mug pour a shot of espresso, fill half full with steamed milk. Add 1 teaspoon of cinnamon; fill almost to the top with steamed milk. Top off with a spoonful of foamed milk, a dusting of cinnamon and a cinnamon stick.

Iced Espresso Drinks

Iced Espresso Drinks

Iced Latte

- 2-3 ounces of espresso
- 1 cup of cold milk

Fill a regular glass with ice, pour a shot of espresso over the ice and fill to the top with cold milk.

Iced Mocha

- 2-3 ounces of espresso

- 3 Tbs of creme de coco
      or
- 3 Tbs of Hershey's syrup

Fill a tall glass half full ice. Pour a single shot of espresso over the ice and add 3 Tbs of creme de cacao or Hershey's syrup. Fill three quarters full with cold milk. Stir and top off with cold milk.

Iced Cafe Royal

- 2-3 ounces of espresso
- 1 cup of Eagle brand milk

Fill a regular glass with ice, pour a shot of espresso over the ice and fill to the top with Eagle brand condensed milk.

Iced Breve

- 2-3 ounces of espresso
- 1 cup of cream

Fill a regular glass with ice, pour a shot of espresso over the ice and top off with cream.

Espresso Float

- 2-3 ounces of espresso
- 1 scoop of ice cream

- 3 Tbs of creme de cacao
  or
- 3 Tbs of Hershey's syrup

An excellent cold dessert in a large coffee mug. Put a scoop of your favorite ice cream and pour a shot of espresso over the ice cream. Top with creme de cacao or Hershey's syrup and whipping cream.

Virgin Drinks (no espresso)

Steamed Milk

Pour steamed milk into a regular coffee mug. Adding your favorite flavored syrup always makes for a better drink. A few suggestions are: vanilla, orgeat, creme de cacao or Hershey's syrup.

Hot Chocolate

The steaming process of the espresso machine creates an excellent hot chocolate. Using whole milk, add 2 Tbs of hot chocolate mix. Steam the milk as usual and pour into coffee mug. Top off with whipping cream and powdered chocolate.

Hot Cider

Pour cold cider into the stainless steel pitcher and add the desired amount of cinnamon, nutmeg and sugar. Place the steam tube to the bottom of the pitcher. Steam until pitcher is too hot to touch, pour into regular coffee mug and garnish with a cinnamon stick.

Your Own Espresso Creations

Your Own Espresso Creations

Your Own Espresso Creations

Your Own Espresso Creations

You are invited to submit your favorite espresso creation to the publisher.

Some recipes will be selected for the next edition of "*Espresso* **Magic**"

All recipes submitted become the property of the publishers.

Send recipes, comments or orders to:

Shady Lane Enterprises
P.O. Box 55942
Lake Forest Park, WA
98155

Share a copy of "*Espresso* **Magic**" with a friend. A great gift. Mail $5.95 plus $1.00 for shipping and handling to Shady Lane Enterprises. Be sure to enclose the mail-to address.

Shady Lane
Enterprises